Practical
Baking

p^3

This is a P³ Book
This edition published in 2004

P³
Queen Street House
4 Queen Street
Bath BA1 1HE, UK

Copyright © Parragon 2002

ISBN: 1-40542-304-8

Manufactured in China

NOTE

Cup measurements in this book are for American cups.
This book also uses imperial and metric measurements. Follow the same units
of measurement throughout; do not mix imperial and metric.
All spoon measurements are level: teaspoons are assumed to be 5 ml, and
tablespoons are assumed to be 15 ml. Unless otherwise stated,
milk is assumed to be whole milk, eggs and individual vegetables such as potatoes
are medium, and pepper is freshly ground black pepper.

The nutritional information provided for each recipe is per serving or per person.
Optional ingredients, variations, or serving suggestions have
not been included in the calculations. The times given for each recipe are an approximate
guide only because the preparation times may differ according to the techniques used by
different people and the cooking times may vary as a result of the type of oven used.

Recipes using raw or very lightly cooked eggs should be
avoided by infants, the elderly, pregnant women, convalescents,
and anyone suffering from an illness.

Contents

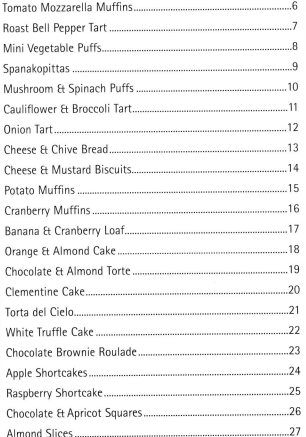

Introduction

Today, when everything is readily available precooked, prepackaged, and always uniform in shape, size, and taste, it can be revitalizing to ring the changes occasionally and do some home baking. Cookies, biscuits, cakes, breads, and even pizzas are quick, easy, and rewarding to make, and your efforts will be much appreciated by family and friends. The tempting cookie recipes included in this book will transform a short break for coffee or tea into an occasion to be lingered over, while slices, sweet and savory, will pack easily into a school lunch-box or a hamper, to be enjoyed on a leisurely picnic. The recipes have been chosen to present a mix of traditional favorites for festivals and occasions, and exciting new ideas to inspire you.

Ingredients

Home baking can be a cost-saver, because ingredients can be very inexpensive. But for the very best results you will need top-quality ingredients. Unbleached flours, unrefined sugars, and free-range eggs can all be found in large stores and food markets. Organically grown produce tends to be high quality and it is now very widely available. Buy genuine vanilla extract instead of the cheaper vanilla flavoring, and good-quality chocolate with a high cocoa-solid content. Items such as spices, nuts, coconut, and dried fruits will keep for

some time in your pantry, but they lose their flavor if they are kept for too long. Update your supplies regularly, especially if you bake rarely or only at irregular intervals.

The ingredient that can make a big difference to the taste and texture of cookies and cakes is fat. Butter may ooze cholesterol, but it is the best type of fat to use.

Stocking the pantry

To maximize their shelf-life, baking ingredients should be stored in airtight tins or jars in a cool, dark place. Ingredients to store include baking powder and baking soda, unsweetened cocoa (not drinking chocolate), ground almonds, pure vanilla extract, and perhaps orange, lemon, and chocolate extract, white and whole-wheat plain and self-rising flours, and a wide variety of sugars, including white and golden superfine sugar, and light and dark raw brown sugars.

A selection of dried fruits such as raisins, golden raisins, dates, cranberries, and currants will always be needed, and dried apricots make a great filling for nutty whole-wheat pastry slices. Jars of crunchy peanut butter, molasses, and honey are other necessary basics. Your spice collection could include a jar of allspice—a ready-made blend of cinnamon, coriander, nutmeg, cloves, and ginger—and individual jars of cinnamon, ginger, ground cloves, and whole nutmegs (the flavor and aroma of freshly grated nutmeg are very special).

Many recipes in this book are for savory cookies and slices, and for these you will need cayenne pepper, paprika, and mustard powder. Mustard brings out the full flavor of sharp cheese.

Unsweetened pie dough is easy to make, but ready-made varieties are excellent, and it is helpful to keep some in the freezer, especially packages of the more difficult phyllo pastry and puff pastry. These ready-made varieties will enable you to make a quick base for some impressive savory tarts and slices without sacrificing quality for speed.

You may occasionally find you need an unexpected ingredient for a particular recipe. For example, one recipe in this book calls for dried lavender flowers, which lend an original aroma and flavor to cookies. Special ingredients like these usually need to be bought as you use them.

Baking methods

Most cakes and biscuits are made by creaming or rubbing-in. The techniques for these, explained below, do not include quantities because these depend on the recipe.

Creaming: fat and sugar are beaten together, either by hand with a wooden spoon or with an electric whisk, until the mixture is pale and creamy; eggs are then added a little at a time, then flour is folded in with a metal spoon: the mixture is turned over gently until all ingredients are blended. It is important not to over-mix, since it is air in the mixture that makes a light cookie.

Rubbing-in: this method is similar to that used for making pie dough. Fat is rubbed into flour with the fingertips until the mixture resembles fine bread crumbs, then sugar, eggs, and other ingredients are added.

Cooking: cake mixtures are transferred to a pan for cooking, usually a round, square, or loaf-shaped one, or the shallow sheet-type, which is ideal for brownies and other slices cut into squares.

Cookie dough may be rolled out and cut into shapes, or placed in spoonfuls at intervals on the cookie sheet and flattened very slightly with the fingers or the back of a spoon. However, they need plenty of room to spread or you will turn out a collection of curiously shaped globs instead of neat rows of separated cookies.

Cookie-cutters come in simple shapes, such as fluted circles, hearts, stars, numbers, and even Christmas trees, so there is wide scope for shaping a batch of cookies for a special occasion and presenting them beautifully.

Handy tips

The recipes in this book are simple to follow, but for the best results, follow them step by step. Before you begin, read and follow these tips:

1. Use the correct ingredients. For example, using a rich, raw, brown sugar in place of a light, white superfine sugar will change the flavor of a cookie.

2. Preheat the oven to the temperature given in the recipe. A fan-assisted oven may need a slightly lower temperature (and a slightly shorter cooking time).

3. Find baking pans of the size and shape specified in the recipe. Grease and line cake pans, and lightly grease baking sheets for cookies, breads, and biscuits. Be sure to prepare enough baking pans or sheets for the size of the batch you plan to cook.

4. Weigh out all the ingredients before you start, assemble them in the order listed in the recipe, and bring chilled items such as fat and eggs to room temperature. Carry out any food preparation, such as chopping, grating, or slicing. Sift flour with any salt, spices, or baking soda to be used, holding the sieve high above the bowl to incorporate air.

5. Put the ingredients together in the order listed in the recipe, and follow the instructions carefully for mixing and blending. Some recipes include chilling in the refrigerator to make the dough easier to handle.

6. Keep an eye on your baking while it is in the oven, but do not open the door until nearly the end of the cooking time. Cakes are cooked when they spring back if touched lightly with a finger, or when a skewer inserted into the center comes out clean. Cookies are cooked when they are lightly colored on top. Breads, biscuits, and pie doughs should be well-risen and golden.

7. Cookies should be lifted very carefully onto a wire rack as soon as they come out of the oven, to let them cool completely. It may be tempting to eat or serve them immediately, but they really need time to crisp up. Some cakes may need to be left in the pan to cool, while others should be turned out onto a wire rack—always be guided by the instructions in the recipe.

KEY	
	Simplicity level 1–3 (1 easiest, 3 slightly harder)
	Preparation time
	Cooking time

Tomato Mozzarella Muffins

These delicious mini pizzas, using English muffins as a ready-made base, can be prepared and cooked in just half an hour.

NUTRITIONAL INFORMATION

Calories	232	Sugars	.........4g
Protein	.........4g	Fat	..........15g
Carbohydrate	...20g	Saturates	.......8g

 5–10 mins 10 mins

SERVES 4

INGREDIENTS

4 large, ripe tomatoes

1 tbsp tomato paste

8 pitted black olives, halved

4 English muffins

4 garlic cloves, crushed

2 tbsp butter

1 tbsp chopped basil

1¾ oz/50 g mozzarella cheese, sliced

salt and pepper

fresh basil leaves, to garnish

DRESSING

1 tbsp olive oil

2 tsp lemon juice

1 tsp clear honey

VARIATION
Use balsamic vinegar instead of the lemon juice for an authentic Italian flavor.

1 Cut a cross shape at the bottom of each tomato. Plunge the tomatoes in a bowl of boiling water—this will make the skin easier to peel. After a few minutes, pick each tomato up with a fork and peel away the skin. Chop the tomato flesh and mix with the tomato paste and olives.

2 Cut the 4 English muffins in half to give eight thick pieces. Toast all the muffin halves under a hot broiler for 2–3 minutes until they have turned a rich golden brown color.

3 Mix the garlic, butter, and basil together and spread onto each muffin half. Top with a generous layer of the tomato and olive mixture.

4 Mix the dressing ingredients and drizzle over each muffin. Arrange the mozzarella cheese on top and season.

5 Return the muffins to the broiler for 1–2 minutes until the cheese melts.

6 Garnish with fresh basil leaves and serve at once.

Roast Bell Pepper Tart

Roasting the vegetables gives this bell pepper tart a delicious originality.
Serve it hot or leave it to cool for outdoor eating.

NUTRITIONAL INFORMATION

Calories	237	Sugars	.........3g
Protein	.........6g	Fat	..........15g
Carbohydrate	...20g	Saturates	.......4g

   25 mins   40 mins

SERVES 8

INGREDIENTS

PIE DOUGH

1¼ cups all-purpose flour

pinch of salt

5 tbsp butter or margarine

2 tbsp finely chopped green pitted olives

3 tbsp cold water

FILLING

1 red bell pepper

1 green bell pepper

1 yellow bell pepper

2 garlic cloves, crushed

2 tbsp olive oil

1 cup grated mozzarella cheese

2 eggs

⅔ cup milk

1 tbsp chopped fresh basil

salt and pepper

1 To make the pie dough, sift the flour and salt into a bowl. Rub in the butter or margarine until the mixture resembles fine bread crumbs. Add the olives and cold water, bringing the mixture together to form a dough.

2 Roll the dough out on a floured counter and use to line an 8-inch/20-cm loose-bottomed tart pan. Prick the bottom with a fork and let chill.

3 Meanwhile, cut all the bell peppers in half lengthwise, seed, and place them, skin side uppermost, on a cookie sheet. Mix together the garlic and oil and brush over the bell peppers. Cook in a preheated oven, 400°F/200°C, for 20 minutes, or until they begin to char slightly. Let the peppers cool slightly and then slice thinly. Arrange them in the pastry shell, and then sprinkle over the mozzarella.

4 Beat together the eggs and milk and add the basil. Season and pour over the peppers. Put the tart on a cookie sheet and bake in the oven for 20 minutes, or until set. Serve hot or cold.

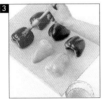

Mini Vegetable Puffs

These puffs look so impressive that they deserve to appear at the start of a formal meal. Yet they are surprisingly quick to make.

NUTRITIONAL INFORMATION

Calories	.... .649	Sugars	.... .3g
Protein	.... .9g	Fat	.... .45g
Carbohydrate	...57g	Saturates	...... .18g

  45 mins   20 mins

SERVES 4

I N G R E D I E N T S

1 lb/450 g puff pastry, defrosted if frozen

1 egg, beaten

F I L L I N G

8 oz/225 g sweet potato, cubed

3½ oz/100 g baby asparagus spears

2 tbsp butter

1 leek, sliced

2 small open-cap mushrooms, sliced

1 tsp lime juice

1 tsp chopped fresh thyme

pinch of dried mustard

salt and pepper

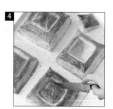

1 Cut the dough into 4 equal pieces. Roll each piece out on a lightly floured counter to form a 5-inch/13-cm square. Place on a dampened cookie sheet and score a smaller 3-inch/7.5-cm square inside each one.

2 Brush with beaten egg and cook in a preheated oven, 400°F/200°C, for 20 minutes, or until the puff pastry is risen and golden brown.

3 Meanwhile, make the filling. Cook the sweet potato in a pan of boiling water for 15 minutes, until tender. Drain well and set aside. Meanwhile, blanch the asparagus in another pan of boiling water for about 10 minutes, or until tender. Drain and reserve.

4 Remove the puff pastry squares from the oven, then carefully cut out the central square from each one with a sharp knife. Lift out and reserve.

5 Melt the butter in a pan, add the leek and mushrooms, and sauté for 2–3 minutes. Add the lime juice, thyme, and mustard, season well with salt and pepper, and stir in the sweet potatoes and asparagus. Spoon the mixture into the pastry shells, top with the reserved puff pastry squares, and serve immediately.

Spanakopittas

These Greek spinach and feta pies, with their layers of crisp phyllo pastry, are ideal to serve as an appetizer or as a light lunchtime dish.

NUTRITIONAL INFORMATION

Calories 952	Sugars 15g
Protein 18g	Fat 61g
Carbohydrate . . .87g	Saturates 29g

40 mins   25 mins

SERVES 4

INGREDIENTS

2 tbsp olive oil

6 scallions, chopped

9 oz/250 g fresh young spinach leaves, tough stems removed, then rinsed

¼ cup long-grain rice (not basmati), boiled until tender and drained

4 tbsp chopped fresh dill

4 tbsp chopped fresh parsley

4 tbsp pine nuts

2 tbsp raisins

generous ½ cup crumbled feta cheese, drained if necessary

¼ nutmeg, freshly grated

pinch of cayenne pepper (optional)

40 sheets phyllo pastry

generous 1 cup melted butter

pepper

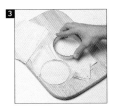

1 Heat the oil in a pan, add the scallions, and cook for about 2 minutes. Add the spinach, with just the water clinging to the leaves, and cook, stirring, until the leaves wilt. Let the vegetables cool a little, then drain off and squeeze out the liquid.

2 Stir the rice, herbs, pine nuts, raisins, feta cheese, and nutmeg into the spinach mixture, and add cayenne pepper and black pepper to taste.

3 Leave the phyllo sheets in a stack. Cut forty 6-inch/15-cm squares. Then cut just eight 4-inch/10-cm circles. Re-wrap the unused dough and cover the cut shapes with a damp dish towel.

4 Brush four 4-inch/10-cm loose-bottomed tart pans with butter. Make the first pie: lay one square of phyllo across a tart pan and brush with butter. Repeat with 9 more sheets.

5 Spoon in one-fourth of the filling and smooth the surface. Top with a phyllo circle and brush with butter. Repeat with another phyllo circle. Fold the over-hanging phyllo over the top and brush with butter. Make 3 more pies in the same way.

6 Put the pies on a cookie sheet and bake in a preheated oven, 350°F/180°C, for 20–25 minutes, until crisp and golden. Let stand for 5 minutes before turning out.

Mushroom & Spinach Puffs

These puffs, filled with garlic, mushrooms, and spinach, are easy to make and they bake to an appealing golden brown.

NUTRITIONAL INFORMATION

Calories ....467 Sugars 4g
Protein ....8g Fat 38g
Carbohydrate ...24g Saturates 18g

25 mins   20 mins

SERVES 4

INGREDIENTS

2 tbsp butter

1 red onion, halved and sliced

2 garlic cloves, crushed

3 cups sliced open-cap mushrooms

6 oz/175 g baby spinach

pinch of nutmeg

4 tbsp heavy cream

8 oz/225 g ready-made puff pastry, defrosted if frozen

1 egg, beaten

2 tsp poppy seeds

salt and pepper

1 Melt the butter in a skillet. Add the onion and garlic and sauté over low heat, stirring, for 3–4 minutes, until the onion has softened.

2 Add the mushrooms, spinach, and nutmeg and then cook them over medium heat, stirring occasionally, for 2–3 minutes.

3 Stir in the heavy cream, mixing thoroughly. Season with salt and pepper to taste and remove the pan from the heat. Set aside.

4 Roll out the dough on a lightly floured counter and cut it into four 6-inch/15-cm circles, using a bowl or a saucer as a guide.

5 Dampen the dough edges with water. Put one fourth of the filling onto one half of each circle and fold the dough over to encase it. Press down to seal the edges and brush with the beaten egg. Sprinkle over the poppy seeds.

6 Place the puffs on a dampened cookie sheet and cook in a preheated oven, 400°F/200°C, for 20 minutes, until risen and golden brown. Serve immediately.

COOK'S TIP

The cookie sheet is dampened so that steam forms with the heat of the oven, which helps the dough to rise and set.

Cauliflower & Broccoli Tart

This tasty tart can be made in a shorter time if you make the pastry shell in advance and keep it frozen until required.

NUTRITIONAL INFORMATION

Calories	252	Sugars	.........3g
Protein	.........7g	Fat	..........16g
Carbohydrate	...22g	Saturates	.......5g

🥧 🥧 🥧

🍳 35 mins   🕐 30 mins

SERVES 8

I N G R E D I E N T S

PASTRY SHELL

1¼ cups all-purpose flour

pinch of salt

½ tsp paprika

1 tsp dried thyme

5 tbsp margarine

3 tbsp water

FILLING

3½ oz/100 g cauliflower florets

3½ oz/100 g broccoli florets

1 onion, cut into eight

2 tbsp butter or margarine

1 tbsp all-purpose flour

6 tbsp vegetable stock

½ cup milk

¾ cup grated colby cheese

salt and pepper

paprika, to garnish

1 To make the pastry shell, sift the flour and salt into a bowl. Add the paprika and thyme and rub in the margarine. Stir in the water and bind to form a dough.

2 Roll out the dough on a floured counter and use to line a 7-inch/18-cm loose-bottomed tart pan. Prick the bottom with a fork and line with baking parchment. Fill with baking beans and bake in a preheated oven, 375°F/190°C, for 15 minutes. Remove the parchment and beans and return the pastry shell to the oven for 5 minutes.

3 To make the filling, put the cauliflower, broccoli, and onion in a pan of lightly salted boiling water and cook for 10–12 minutes, until tender. Drain and reserve.

4 Melt the butter in a pan. Add the flour and cook, stirring constantly, for 1 minute. Remove from the heat, stir in the stock and milk, and return to the heat. Bring to a boil, stirring, and add ½ cup of the cheese. Season to taste with salt and pepper.

5 Spoon the cauliflower, broccoli, and onion into the pastry shell. Pour over the sauce and sprinkle with the remaining cheese. Return to the oven for 10 minutes, until the cheese is bubbling. Dust with paprika and serve.

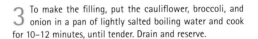

Onion Tart

This crisp pie shell is filled with a tasty mixture of onions and cheese and baked to a perfect crispness.

NUTRITIONAL INFORMATION

Calories	394	Sugars	.........7g
Protein	........11g	Fat	.........27g
Carbohydrate	...29g	Saturates	......12g

  45 mins   30 mins

SERVES 4

INGREDIENTS

9 oz/250 g ready-made short pastry, defrosted if frozen

3 tbsp butter

2³⁄₄ oz/75 g bacon, chopped

1lb 9 oz/700 g onions, peeled and thinly sliced

2 eggs, beaten

¹⁄₂ cup freshly grated Parmesan cheese

1 tsp dried sage

salt and pepper

1 Roll out the dough on a lightly floured counter and use to line the bottom and sides of a 9¹⁄₂-inch/24-cm loose-bottomed tart pan.

2 Prick the dough with a fork and let chill in the refrigerator for 30 minutes.

3 Meanwhile, melt the butter in a pan, add the chopped bacon and sliced onions, and cook them over low heat for about 25 minutes, stirring occasionally, until tender. If the onion starts to brown, add 1 tablespoon of water to the pan. Let cool slightly.

4 Add the beaten eggs to the onion mixture, stir in the grated cheese and sage, and season with salt and pepper to taste.

5 Spoon the bacon and onion mixture into the prepared pastry shell.

6 Bake in a preheated oven, 350°F/180°C, for about 20–30 minutes, or until the filling has just set firm and the pastry is crisp and golden.

7 Let the cooked tart cool slightly in the pan, then serve it warm or cold.

VARIATION

For a vegetarian version of this tart, replace the bacon with the same amount of chopped mushrooms.

Cheese & Chive Bread

This is a quick bread full of cheese flavor. To enjoy it at its best, eat it as soon as it cools after emerging from the oven.

NUTRITIONAL INFORMATION

Calories .... 190 Sugars 1g
Protein .... 7g Fat 9g
Carbohydrate ... 22g Saturates 5g

 20 mins 🕐 30 mins

SERVES 8

INGREDIENTS

butter, for greasing

generous 1½ cups self-rising flour

1 tsp salt

1 tsp mustard powder

1 cup grated sharp cheese

2 tbsp chopped fresh chives

1 egg, beaten

2 tbsp butter, melted

²⁄₃ cup milk

1 Grease a 9-inch/23-cm square cake pan with a little butter and line the bottom with baking parchment.

2 Sift the flour, salt, and mustard powder into a large mixing bowl.

3 Reserve 3 tablespoons of the grated cheese and stir the remainder into the flour mixture, together with the chopped fresh chives.

4 Add the beaten egg, melted butter, and milk to the dry ingredients and stir the mixture thoroughly to combine.

5 Transfer the mixture to the prepared cake pan and spread it over evenly with a knife. Sprinkle over the reserved grated cheese.

6 Bake in a preheated oven, 375°F/190°C, for 30 minutes.

7 Remove from the oven and let the bread cool slightly in the pan. Turn out onto a wire rack to cool completely. Cut into triangles to serve.

COOK'S TIP

You can use other fresh herbs, such as thyme, rosemary, and basil, in this recipe.

Cheese & Mustard Biscuits

Mustard accentuates the taste of grated sharp cheese to give these homemade biscuits greater intensity of flavor.

NUTRITIONAL INFORMATION

Calories	218	Sugars	. . . . .1g
Protein	. . . . .7g	Fat	. . . . .12g
Carbohydrate	. . .22g	Saturates	. . . . . .7g

 15 mins   15 mins

MAKES 8

I N G R E D I E N T S

4 tbsp butter, cut into small pieces, plus extra for greasing

generous 1½ cups self-rising flour

1 tsp baking powder

pinch of salt

1 cup grated sharp cheese

1 tsp mustard powder

⅔ cup milk

pepper

1 Grease a cookie sheet lightly with a little butter.

2 Sift the flour, baking powder, and salt into a mixing bowl. Rub in the remaining butter with your fingertips until the mixture resembles fine bread crumbs.

3 Stir in the grated cheese, mustard, and enough milk to form a soft dough.

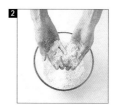

COOK'S TIP

Biscuits should be eaten on the day they are made because they quickly go stale. Serve them split in half and spread with butter.

4 On a lightly floured counter, knead the dough very lightly, then flatten it out with the palm of your hand to a circle about 1 inch/2.5 cm thick.

5 Cut the dough into 8 wedges with a knife. Brush each one with a little milk and sprinkle with pepper to taste.

6 Place the wedges on a cookie sheet. Bake in a preheated oven, 425°F/220°C, for 10–15 minutes, until the biscuits are golden brown.

7 Transfer the biscuits to a wire rack and let cool slightly. Serve them while they are still warm.

Potato Muffins

These light-textured muffins rise like little soufflés in the oven and are best eaten warm. The dried fruit can be varied according to taste.

NUTRITIONAL INFORMATION

Calories	98	Sugars	........11g
Protein	.........3g	Fat	...........2g
Carbohydrate	...18g	Saturates	.....0.5g

🥧 30 mins   🕐 20 mins

SERVES 4

INGREDIENTS

4 tsp melted butter, for greasing

½ cup self-rising flour, plus extra for dusting

1½ cups mealy potatoes, peeled and diced

2 tbsp brown sugar

1 tsp baking powder

generous ¾ cup raisins

4 eggs, separated

1 Lightly grease 12 cups in a muffin pan with butter and dust with flour.

2 Cook the diced potatoes in a pan of boiling water for 10 minutes, or until tender. Drain well and mash until completely smooth.

3 Transfer the mashed potatoes to a mixing bowl and add the flour, sugar, baking powder, raisins, and egg yolks. Stir well to mix thoroughly.

4 In a clean bowl, whisk the egg whites until standing in peaks. Using a metal spoon, gently fold them into the potato mixture until fully blended.

5 Divide the mixture between the prepared pans.

6 Cook in a preheated oven, 400°F/200°C, for 10 minutes. Lower the oven temperature to 325°F/160°C and cook the muffins for an additional 7–10 minutes, or until risen.

7 Remove the muffins from the pans and serve warm.

COOK'S TIP

Instead of spreading the muffins with plain butter, serve them with cinnamon butter made by blending ¼ cup butter with a large pinch of ground cinnamon.

Cranberry Muffins

These savory muffins are an ideal accompaniment to soup, and they make a nice change from sweet cakes for serving with coffee.

NUTRITIONAL INFORMATION

Calories	96	Sugars	.........4g
Protein	.........3g	Fat	...........4g
Carbohydrate	...14g	Saturates	.......2g

  25 mins   20 mins

MAKES 18

INGREDIENTS

2 tsp melted butter, for greasing

generous 1½ cups all-purpose flour

2 tsp baking powder

½ tsp salt

3 tbsp superfine sugar

4 tbsp butter, melted

2 eggs, beaten

generous ¾ cup milk

1 cup fresh cranberries

generous ¼ cup freshly grated
   Parmesan cheese

1 Lightly grease 18 cups in two 12-cup muffin pans with butter. Sift the flour, baking powder, and salt into a mixing bowl. Stir in the superfine sugar.

2 In a separate bowl, mix the butter, beaten eggs, and milk together. Pour into the bowl of dry ingredients. Mix lightly together until all of the ingredients are evenly combined. Finally, stir in the fresh cranberries.

3 Divide the cake batter between the prepared muffin pans. Sprinkle the grated Parmesan cheese over the top of each muffin.

4 Bake in a preheated oven, 400°F/200°C, for about 20 minutes, or until the muffins are well risen and a golden brown color.

5 Remove from the oven and let the muffins cool a little in the pans, then carefully transfer them onto a wire rack. Let them cool completely before transferring to a plate and serving.

VARIATION

For a sweet alternative to this recipe, replace the Parmesan cheese with raw brown sugar in step 3, if you prefer.

Banana & Cranberry Loaf

Chopped nuts, mixed rind, fresh orange juice, and dried cranberries all contribute to the moist richness of this fruit bread.

NUTRITIONAL INFORMATION

Calories ....388 Sugars 40g
Protein ....5g Fat 17g
Carbohydrate ...57g Saturates 2g

  10 mins   1 hr

SERVES 8

INGREDIENTS

butter, for greasing

1½ cups self-rising flour

½ tsp baking powder

¾ cup soft brown sugar

2 bananas, mashed

2–3 tbsp chopped mixed citrus rind

3 tbsp chopped mixed nuts

⅓ cup dried cranberries

5–6 tbsp orange juice

2 eggs, beaten

⅔ cup sunflower oil

5 tbsp confectioners' sugar, sifted

zest of 1 orange, grated

1 Grease a 2-lb/900-g loaf pan with butter and line the bottom with baking parchment.

2 Sift the flour and baking powder into a bowl. Stir in the sugar, bananas, mixed rind, nuts, and dried cranberries.

3 In a separate bowl, stir the orange juice, eggs, and sunflower oil together until well combined. Add the mixture to the dry ingredients and mix until well blended. Spoon the mixture into the prepared loaf pan and smooth the top.

4 Bake in a preheated oven, 350°F/180°C, for about 1 hour until firm to the touch, or until a fine skewer inserted into the center comes out clean.

5 Turn the loaf out of the pan and let cool on a wire rack.

6 Mix the confectioners' sugar with a little water and drizzle the frosting over the loaf. Sprinkle over the orange zest. Let the frosting set before slicing and serving.

COOK'S TIP

This fruit bread will keep for a couple of days. Wrap it carefully and store it in a cool, dry place.

Orange & Almond Cake

This light and tangy citrus cake from Sicily is better eaten as a dessert than as a cake. It is especially good served after a large meal.

NUTRITIONAL INFORMATION

Calories ....399 Sugars 20g
Protein ....8g Fat 31g
Carbohydrate ...23g Saturates 13g

25 mins   40 mins

SERVES 8

INGREDIENTS

melted butter, for greasing

4 eggs, separated

⅔ cup superfine sugar, plus 2 tsp for the cream

finely grated zest and juice of 2 oranges

finely grated zest and juice of 1 lemon

generous 1 cup ground almonds

scant ¼ cup self-rising flour

generous ¾ cup light cream, for whipping

1 tsp cinnamon

scant ¼ cup slivered almonds, toasted

confectioners' sugar, to dust

1 Grease and line the bottom of a 7-inch/18-cm round, deep cake pan.

2 Whisk the egg yolks with the sugar until thick and creamy. Whisk in half the orange zest and all the lemon zest.

VARIATION

You could serve this cake with a syrup. Boil the juice and finely grated zest of 2 oranges, 6 tbsp superfine sugar, and 2 tbsp of water for 5–6 minutes, until slightly thickened. Stir in 1 tbsp of orange liqueur just before serving.

3 Mix the orange and lemon juice with the ground almonds and stir into the egg yolk mixture. It will become quite runny at this point. Fold in the flour.

4 Whisk the egg whites until stiff and gently fold into the egg yolk mixture.

5 Pour the cake mixture into the pan and bake the cake in a preheated oven, at 350°F/180°C, for 35–40 minutes, or until golden and springy to the touch. Let the cake cool in the pan for 10 minutes

and then turn it out. The cake is likely to sink slightly at this stage.

6 Whip the cream to form soft peaks. Stir in the remaining orange zest, the cinnamon, and the 2 teaspoons of sugar.

7 Once the cake is cold, cover with the almonds, dust with confectioners' sugar, and serve with the cream.

Chocolate & Almond Torte

This torte is perfect for serving on a hot, sunny day with cream and a selection of fresh summer berries.

NUTRITIONAL INFORMATION

Calories 399	Sugars 30g	
Protein 5g	Fat 28g	
Carbohydrate . . .36g	Saturates 14g	

🍰 30 mins   ⏱ 45 mins

SERVES 10

INGREDIENTS

¾ cup butter, softened, plus extra for greasing

8 oz/225 g bittersweet chocolate, broken into pieces

3 tbsp water

¾ cup brown sugar

¼ cup ground almonds

3 tbsp self-rising flour

5 eggs, separated

¾ cup finely chopped blanched almonds

confectioners' sugar, for dusting

heavy cream, to serve (optional)

1 Grease a 9-inch/23-cm loose bottomed cake pan with butter and line the bottom with baking parchment.

2 In a pan set over very low heat, melt the chocolate with the water, stirring until smooth. Add the sugar and stir until dissolved. Remove from the heat to prevent overheating.

3 Add the remaining butter in small amounts until it has melted into the chocolate. Lightly stir in the ground almonds and flour. Add the egg yolks one at a time, beating well after each addition.

4 Whisk the egg whites until they stand in soft peaks, then fold them into the chocolate mixture with a metal spoon. Stir in the chopped almonds. Pour the mixture into the cake pan and level the surface.

5 Bake in a preheated oven, 350°F/180°C, for 40–45 minutes, until well risen and firm (the cake will crack on the surface during cooking).

6 Let cool in the pan for 30–40 minutes. Turn out onto a wire rack to cool completely. Dust with confectioners' sugar and serve in slices, with cream if using.

COOK'S TIP
For a nuttier flavor, toast the chopped almonds in a dry skillet over medium heat for 2 minutes, until lightly golden.

Clementine Cake

This cake is flavored with clementine rind and juice, filling its rich, buttery slices with fresh fruit flavor.

NUTRITIONAL INFORMATION

Calories . . . . . . .427 Sugars 32g
Protein . . . . .6g Fat 25g
Carbohydrate . . .48g Saturates 13g

35 mins   1 hour

SERVES 8

INGREDIENTS

¾ cup butter (softened), plus extra
  for greasing

2 clementines

generous ¾ cup superfine sugar

3 eggs, beaten

1¼ cups self-rising flour

3 tbsp ground almonds

3 tbsp light cream

GLAZE AND TOPPING

6 tbsp clementine juice

2 tbsp superfine sugar

3 white sugar cubes, crushed

1 Grease a round 7-inch/18-cm cake pan with butter and line the bottom with baking parchment.

2 Pare the rind from the clementines and chop it finely. In a bowl, cream the remaining butter with the sugar until pale and fluffy. Add the clementine rind.

3 Gradually add the beaten eggs to the mixture, beating thoroughly after each addition.

4 Gently fold in the self-rising flour, followed by the ground almonds and the light cream. Spoon the cake batter into the prepared cake pan.

5 Bake in a preheated oven, 350°F/180°C, for 55–60 minutes, or until a fine skewer inserted into the center comes out clean. Leave the cake in the pan to cool a little.

6 Meanwhile, make the glaze for the cake. Pour the clementine juice into a small pan and add the superfine sugar. Bring the mixture to a boil and simmer for 5 minutes.

7 Transfer the cake to a plate or wire rack. Drizzle the glaze over the cake until it has all been absorbed, and sprinkle with the crushed sugar cubes.

Torta del Cielo

This almond-flavored sponge cake has a dense, moist texture, which melts in the mouth. The perfect accompaniment to a good, strong cup of coffee.

NUTRITIONAL INFORMATION

Calories	795	Sugars	........46g
Protein	........14g	Fat	..........51g
Carbohydrate	...76g	Saturates	......23g

 25 mins   50 mins

SERVES 4–6

I N G R E D I E N T S

1 cup sweet butter (at room temperature), plus extra for greasing

1¼ cups raw almonds (in their skins)

1 cup sugar, plus 2 tbsp

3 eggs, lightly beaten

1 tsp almond extract

1 tsp vanilla extract

½ cup all-purpose flour

pinch of salt

T O   S E R V E

confectioners' sugar, for dusting

slivered almonds, toasted

1 Lightly grease a round or square 8-inch/20-cm cake pan with butter and line with baking parchment.

2 Place the almonds in a food processor and grind to a crumbly consistency.

3 In a bowl, beat together the butter and sugar until smooth and fluffy. Beat in the almonds, eggs, and almond and vanilla extracts. Blend well.

4 Stir in the flour and salt, and mix together briefly, until the flour is just incorporated.

5 Pour or spoon the cake batter into the greased pan and smooth the surface. Bake in a preheated oven at 350°F/180°C for 40–50 minutes, or until the cake feels spongy when pressed.

6 Remove the pan from the oven, and put on a wire rack to cool completely. To serve, dust the cake with confectioners' sugar and decorate with the toasted slivered almonds.

White Truffle Cake

A light white sponge, topped with a rich creamy-white chocolate truffle mixture, makes an out-of-this-world treat.

NUTRITIONAL INFORMATION

Calories	358	Sugars	........26g
Protein	.........6g	Fat	..........25g
Carbohydrate	...29g	Saturates	......15g

40 mins, plus chilling   25 mins

SERVES 12

I N G R E D I E N T S

butter, for greasing

2 eggs

¼ cup superfine sugar

6 tbsp all-purpose flour

1¾ oz/50 g white chocolate, melted

T R U F F L E   T O P P I N G

1¼ cups heavy cream

12 oz/350 g white chocolate, broken
  into pieces

generous 1 cup Quark or mascarpone

T O   D E C O R A T E

12 oz/350 g semisweet, milk, or white
  chocolate curls (see step 4, below)

unsweetened cocoa, for dusting

1 Grease a round 8-inch/20-cm springform pan and line the bottom.

2 Whisk the eggs and sugar in a bowl for 10 minutes, or until very light and foamy, and the whisk leaves a trail that lasts a few seconds after it is lifted out. Sift the flour and fold into the eggs with a metal spoon. Add the melted white chocolate. Pour the cake batter into the pan and bake in a preheated oven, 350°F/180°C, for 25 minutes, or until springy. Let cool slightly, then transfer to a wire rack until cold. Return the cake to the pan.

3 To make the topping, place the cream in a pan and bring to a boil, stirring constantly. Cool slightly, then add the white chocolate and stir until melted and combined. Remove from the heat and set aside until almost cool, stirring, then mix in the soft cheese. Pour on top of the cake and chill for 2 hours.

4 To make the chocolate curls, pour melted chocolate onto a marble or acrylic board and spread thinly with a spatula. Let it set. Using a scraper, push through the chocolate at a 25° angle until a large curl forms. Chill each curl until set, and then use to decorate the cake. Sprinkle with unsweetened cocoa.

Chocolate Brownie Roulade

This delicious dessert is inspired by chocolate brownies. The addition of nuts and raisins gives it extra texture.

NUTRITIONAL INFORMATION

Calories 436	Sugars 38g	
Protein 7g	Fat 30g	
Carbohydrate ...38g	Saturates 16g	

 45 mins · 25 mins

SERVES 8

INGREDIENTS

2 tsp melted butter, for greasing

5½ oz/150 g semisweet chocolate, broken into pieces

3 tbsp water

generous ¾ cup superfine sugar

5 eggs, separated

scant ¼ cup raisins, chopped

scant ¼ cup pecans, chopped

pinch of salt

confectioners' sugar, for dusting

1¼ cups heavy cream, lightly whipped

1 Grease a 12 x 8-inch/30 x 20-cm jelly roll pan with butter, line with baking parchment, and grease the parchment.

2 Place the chocolate, with the water, in a small pan over low heat, stirring until the chocolate has just melted. Let cool a little.

3 In a bowl, whisk the sugar and egg yolks for 2–3 minutes with an electric whisk, until thick and pale. Fold in the cooled chocolate, raisins, and pecans.

4 In a separate bowl, whisk the egg whites with the salt. Fold one fourth of the egg whites into the chocolate mixture, then fold in the rest of the whites, working lightly and quickly.

5 Transfer the cake batter to the prepared pan and bake in a preheated oven, 350°F/180°C, for 25 minutes, until risen and just firm to the touch. Let cool before covering with a sheet of nonstick baking parchment and a damp, clean dish towel. Let the cake stand until completely cold before filling and rolling.

6 Turn onto another piece of baking parchment dusted with confectioners' sugar. Remove the lining parchment.

7 Spread the whipped cream over the roulade. Starting from a short end, roll the sponge away from you, using the paper as a guide. Trim the ends of the roulade to a neat finish and transfer to a serving plate. Let the roulade chill in the refrigerator until ready to serve. Dust with a little more confectioners' sugar.

Apple Shortcakes

This dessert is a sweet biscuit, split and filled with sliced apples and whipped cream. The shortcakes can be eaten warm or cold.

NUTRITIONAL INFORMATION

Calories 511	Sugars 44g
Protein 5g	Fat 24g
Carbohydrate . . .73g	Saturates 15g

🍰 50 mins   🕐 15 mins

SERVES 4

I N G R E D I E N T S

2 tbsp butter (chilled and cut into small pieces), plus extra for greasing

generous 1 cup all-purpose flour

½ tsp salt

1 tsp baking powder

1 tbsp superfine sugar

3 tbsp milk

confectioners' sugar, for dusting (optional)

F I L L I N G

3 dessert apples, peeled, cored, and sliced

½ cup superfine sugar

1 tbsp lemon juice

1 tsp ground cinnamon

1¼ cups water

⅔ cup heavy cream, lightly whipped

1 Lightly grease a cookie sheet. Sift the flour, salt, and baking powder into a mixing bowl. Stir in the sugar, then rub in the butter with your fingers until the mixture resembles fine bread crumbs.

2 Add the milk and mix to a soft dough. On a floured counter, knead the dough. Roll out to ½ inch/1 cm thick. Stamp out 4 circles with a 2-inch/5-cm cookie cutter. Transfer to the prepared cookie sheet.

3 Bake in a preheated oven, 425°F/220°C, for about 15 minutes, until well risen and lightly browned. Remove from the oven and let cool.

4 To make the filling, place the apple, sugar, lemon juice, cinnamon, and water in a pan. Bring to a boil and simmer, uncovered, for 5–10 minutes, until the fruit is tender. Let cool a little. Remove the apples from the pan.

5 To serve, split the four shortcakes in half. Place each bottom half on an individual serving plate and divide the apple slices between the 4 halves, followed by the cream. Place the other halves of the shortcake on top of the cream. Serve either warm or cold, dusted with confectioners' sugar if using.

Raspberry Shortcake

For this lovely summery dessert, two crisp circles of shortbread are sandwiched together with fresh raspberries and lightly whipped cream.

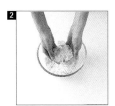  

NUTRITIONAL INFORMATION

Calories ...... .496	Sugars 14g
Protein 4g	Fat 41g
Carbohydrate ...30g	Saturates ..... .26g

15 mins   15 mins

SERVES 8

INGREDIENTS

scant ½ cup butter (cut into cubes), plus extra for greasing

1¼ cups self-rising flour

6 tbsp superfine sugar

1 egg yolk

1 tbsp rose water

2½ cups whipping cream, lightly whipped

2 cups raspberries, plus a few extra for decoration

TO DECORATE

confectioners' sugar

mint leaves

1 Lightly grease 2 cookie sheets with a little butter.

2 To make the shortcake, sift the flour into a bowl. Rub the butter into the flour with your fingers, until the mixture resembles bread crumbs.

3 Stir the sugar, egg yolk, and rose water into the mixture. With your fingers, form a soft dough. Divide the dough into two equal portions.

4 On a lightly floured counter, roll each piece of dough into an 8-inch/20-cm circle. Carefully lift each one with the rolling pin and put onto one of the prepared cookie sheets. Crimp the edges of the dough.

5 Bake in a preheated oven, 375°F/190°C, for 15 minutes, until lightly golden. Transfer the shortcakes to a wire rack and let cool completely.

6 Mix the whipped cream with the raspberries and spoon the mixture on top of one of the shortcakes, spreading it out evenly. Top with the other shortcake circle, dust with a little confectioners' sugar, and decorate with the extra raspberries and mint leaves.

COOK'S TIP
The shortcake can be made without the filling a few days in advance and stored in an airtight container until required.

Chocolate & Apricot Squares

The inclusion of white chocolate makes this a very rich cake, so serve it cut into small squares or bars, or thinly sliced.

NUTRITIONAL INFORMATION

Calories 295	Sugars 23g
Protein 6g	Fat 15g
Carbohydrate ...36g	Saturates 9g

🍫 30 mins 🕐 30 mins

SERVES 12

INGREDIENTS

½ cup butter, plus extra for greasing

6 oz/175 g white chocolate, chopped

4 eggs

⅔ cup superfine sugar

scant 1½ cups all-purpose flour, sifted

1 tsp baking powder

pinch of salt

²/₃ cup no-soak chopped dried apricots

1 Lightly grease a square 9-inch/ 23-cm cake pan with butter and line the bottom with baking parchment.

2 Melt the butter and chocolate in a heatproof bowl set over a pan of simmering water. Stir the mixture frequently with a wooden spoon until it is smooth and glossy. Let cool slightly.

3 Beat the eggs and superfine sugar into the butter and chocolate mixture until well combined.

4 Fold in the flour, baking powder, salt, and chopped dried apricots. Mix together well.

5 Pour the mixture into the prepared cake pan and bake in an oven preheated to 180°C/350°F, for between 25–30 minutes.

6 Remove the cake from the oven. The center may not be completely firm, but it will set as it cools. Let cool in the pan.

7 When the cake is completely cold, turn it out and slice it into small squares or bars.

VARIATION

Replace the white chocolate with milk chocolate or semisweet chocolate, if you prefer.

Almond Slices

A mouthwatering dessert that is sure to impress your guests, especially if it is served with whipped cream.

NUTRITIONAL INFORMATION

Calories 416   Sugars 37g
Protein . . . . .11g   Fat 26g
Carbohydrate . . .38g   Saturates 12g

 15 mins   45 mins

SERVES 8

I N G R E D I E N T S

½ cup sweet butter, plus extra for greasing

⅔ cup ground almonds

1½ cups milk powder

1 cup superfine sugar

½ tsp saffron strands

3 eggs, beaten

scant ¼ cup slivered almonds, to decorate

1 Lightly grease a shallow 9-inch/ 23-cm ovenproof dish with butter.

2 Place the ground almonds, milk powder, sugar, and saffron in a large mixing bowl and stir to mix well.

3 Melt the butter in a small pan. Pour the melted butter over the dry ingredients and mix well.

COOK'S TIP

These almond slices are best eaten hot, but they may also be served cold. They can be made a day or even a week in advance and reheated. They also freeze beautifully.

4 Add the beaten eggs to the mixture and stir to blend well.

5 Spread the cake mixture in the prepared dish and bake in a preheated oven, 325°F/160°C, for 45 minutes. Test whether the cake is cooked through by piercing with the tip of a sharp knife or a

skewer—it will come out clean if it is cooked thoroughly. If not, cook for an additional 5 minutes and test again.

6 Cut the almond cake into slices. Decorate the almond slices with slivered almonds and transfer to serving plates. Serve hot or cold.

Chocolate Chip Brownies

Choose a good-quality chocolate for these chocolate chip brownies to give them a rich flavor that is not too sweet.

NUTRITIONAL INFORMATION

Calories	410	Sugars	.......24g
Protein	.........7g	Fat	.........27g
Carbohydrate	...38g	Saturates	......15g

🍫 20 mins   🕐 35 mins

MAKES 12

INGREDIENTS

1 cup butter, softened, plus extra for greasing

5½ oz/150 g bittersweet chocolate, broken into pieces

generous 1½ cups self-rising flour

⅔ cup superfine sugar

4 eggs, beaten

⅔ cup chopped pistachio nuts

3½ oz/100 g white chocolate, coarsely chopped

confectioners' sugar, for dusting

1 Lightly grease a 9-inch/23-cm square baking pan with butter, and line the bottom with baking parchment.

2 Melt the bittersweet chocolate and butter together in a heatproof bowl set over a pan of simmering water. Let the mixture cool slightly.

3 Sift the flour into a large mixing bowl and stir in the superfine sugar.

4 Stir the eggs into the melted chocolate mixture, then pour this mixture into the flour and sugar mixture, beating well. Stir in the pistachio nuts and white chocolate, then pour the mixture into the pan, using a spatula to spread it evenly into the corners.

5 Bake in a preheated oven, 350°F/180°C, for 30–35 minutes Remove from the oven. Let cool in the pan for 20 minutes, then turn the brownies out onto a wire rack.

6 Dust with confectioners' sugar and cut into 12 pieces when cold.

COOK'S TIP

The brownie will not be completely firm in the middle when it is removed from the oven, but it will set when it has cooled.